More Praise for Punish honey

"In *Punish honey*, an intense felicity of sound leads through
musical abandonment again and again to startling location and
revelation. Fleet, sassy and ferocious, metaphors may turn back
and bite you as well as provide metaphysical, meditative clari-
ties. What dire playfulness, what sexy sting, what headlong
disarrays and arrivals! Reader, here is the real hive."
—DEAN YOUNG

"'Behold hope as an insect bitch, golden bones / for legs,'
Anderson writes in one of the poems of *Punish honey*. Behold,
further, language itself turned more malleable and yet used
more demandingly than in any other book of poems I know.
To say this is a worthy descendant of Maeterlinck is not going
too far. Margaret Cavendish, too, lives on in this work, this
gorgeous display of mind and matter in language. Brilliance
is an apt term for what happens here, for the book's method
as well as its surface." —BIN RAMKE

"Karen Leona Anderson's work is dense and darkly brilliant,
and to appreciate it you will have to be willing to get a little
dirty. She writes out of the tradition of Gertrude Stein, so it's
easy to stub a toe or bang your forehead on parts of speech,
especially small indefinite articles that turn out, after you've
rushed past them, to be bearing the weight of actual nouns or
verbs, leaving you empty-handed and unprepared to make it
to the end of her lines, which meanwhile maintain a very high
velocity, powered by a post-Dickinsonian swiftness that has
shortened Dickinson's dash down into a hyphen, hitching
words together in slippery neologism.

"*Punish honey* revolves around a masterful investigation of a
double resonance in the word 'bee' with two ee's: not just the
creatures, but also the 'bee' of the quilting bee, 'bee' derived
from a dialect English for boon, for unpaid help in manual

labor—the bee of quilting bees, yes, but also a whole variety of group activity, including some pretty ugly things. This not to say the poems aren't beautiful: indeed their beauty shines out critically on page after page. Though they are written in the scene of the sump, where deadly liquids pool, the poems also encompass a whole landscape, a whole world, of folksong and folk medicine, of gorgeously crumpled fabric and bright defiant wit." —CHRIS NEALON

Punish honey

Karen Leona Anderson

Poetry Series #12

CAROLINA WREN PRESS
Durham, North Carolina

Editor: David Kellogg
Series Editor: Andrea Selch

Design: Lesley Landis Designs
Cover Image: "Glow Hive" © 2008 Adam Makarenko
Author Photograph: Jerry Gabriel

The mission of Carolina Wren Press is to seek out, nurture and pro-mote literary work by new and underrepresented writers, including women and writers of color.

Carolina Wren Press is a 501(c)3 non-profit organization supported in part by grants and generous individual donors. In addition, we gratefully acknowledge the ongoing support of Carolina Wren Press's activities made possible through gifts to the Durham Arts Council's United Arts Fund.

Library of Congress Cataloguing-in-Publication Data

Anderson, Karen, 1973-
Punish honey / by Karen Leona Anderson.
    p. cm. -- (Poetry series ; #12)
ISBN 978-0-932112-58-3
I. Title. II. Series.

PS3601.N54425P86 2009
811'.6--dc22

2008050518

FOR JERRY

Table of Contents

THE ANIMAL PARLIAMENT

In vain to punish Honey—
It only sweeter grows—

—*Emily Dickinson*

TULIPS

GORDON COOPER

Blasted with the green of summer and spring combined
        and I, full of every grey the world could provide,
moved thing by thing to the radio station and sang or sing
      all the songs like "Yes I am the One Who is Sobbing"
        I could think of.

How many times can one be said no to, I longed to say;
      as in the movies, I was a fathead full of pain. She looks
        around,
sees nothing but me, and yet I was a perfect choice for the late
        spring, okay,
      cultivar but thick and green, filling the back space,

which she left thing by rattle-brained thing, I now see.
      Because I wanted it, it should find me. The song used to go.
A certain economy, it found me though I wanted it not,
      now sing the sweet, cracked lushness of her bric-a-brac
        and fringed chairs

swept notorious through the High Street. In a van the world departs.
      Will you—is how I know it starts. And ends yes yes or oh.

IRIS
for Amy

Good are the days of the snow
lumped and cupped in the branches
for the slow-toed, jostled green grass,

and but for sun and rain's oily everywhere,
weather might be heavenly arrested, the diner girl
stunning her suitors off with her one-bare-foot

smokebreak always just past,
and barring the cellulose drain
to some plump other face, she were

the world's hard last for its green shoe:
sleek, then brown and slumped, then black.
As good if not good, my iris, breaking all

the stuff around it into sugar and air
in a brief talking-back to the dresses,
gloves, darts, fabric slack and then puffed,

pumped taut with a waste of divisible
flesh; then, we would be the custom,
and if only loose change in the sun's

golden sump, or too slow for the soft
green tips, we are better than dead
in that we are this: breasts, soles, heels, lips.

PARADE
after "The Secret Diary of William Byrd"

The sun rose up for me and so I danced my dance
and made my way to the open platz,

the money-spinning men in place
and free hands all over the sun-glassed maids;

a scene so natural the chance to find
my Snowdrop was slim among the 'What grand breeches!'

and 'How hard it is not to buy a tiger';

sun vellum-thin and silver behind the clouds
and like her name it was Snow because of the color she wore

and Drop for the shape of head or maybe in the way
she fell away and somehow knit together again;

and the crowd outspread across the square
like a new cured pelt and then for me

the parade began and the glasses made
a silver weave around the self-made man emcee,

here to please our eyes and Snowdrop,
broken-necked, helpless-handed queen;

up there I mean, but to say she made the walls
of this constrained and paid-for rendezvous

is to say I danced a dance in a small and wooden room.

RED GEORGETTE

Detached and with sighs, the spring comes,
carefully beading flower's leaves and

of course the brutal pairs of delicate, bloody-
nerve new, dogs stringing and beating between

certain promenade legs. But oh everyone at home and not at home

thinks of radio, video, movie-screen red, happy, lucky-
bodied girl washing out everything bright in park and lot

until it comes in line with the scheme, and that it were
fame she makes a prize of stones and black,

fantastically sleek curls, as if the threat were sheer
sensory meanness, sitting in however rich a car

for four dark months of evenings, and still the front-seat
tussle, the fallow, agonized you-are-the-best. Some teens,

purple crocuses crack open and tell her, like this,
with a late overlay of being trampled and torn.

But the red dress stays true, tacky as it was in mind
and form, with its flames at the sleeves, shirred front

like rust on iridescent skin, for all the world
like something to step out of, but that it didn't get,

and withered, there was no one for or nor her next winter,
just an impatience of new girls to wear the scuffed-up dirt

to something serene and khaki, pants undone and grass
sprung back from the snow to say oh who?

PARTY

The sun's fat soul
has settled in the cold, our yards choked
with the white this morning, and
no morning like a bruised-foot morning
says the something that spatters from our cells
silk-thin, bacon hot. Don't drop
last night's dress because there's nothing
left to drop. Confetti a blindness
coming on and whitely on
my lump-of-mud body, something I start,
my heave-ho only, my cooked goose party.
Maybe I won't—there is no party
that a holy ghost party won't stop.

MONTE CARLO

I'll tell you of all the greatest money-making schemes was the stand
for green tea and the bedroom-cum-whirlpool, notwithstanding
how the wood rotted or having to use the rotting outdoor latrines;
how they attracted the landed gentlemen I can't say or what became
of all the floating long-beaked birds we think of now when we
remember the wallpaper curled from the walls or the heavy thrown
cups cold against the steam of samples: cheap jade water heated to
a bitter howl the way down, then a relative, clean-feeling peace.

And Mother helped in no way, though she seemed to be ladling
when the men were around—here with a cup, here with a towel—
tannin from the walls streaming down them in tea-colored streams;
here was the money part, I guess she said, and held some; thus in
the cup had been my room. I had somehow erred: they had estates
with two lamps to every snake, the gentlemen; they had warmth to
spend and guns lovely for the drowning birds; they had paid, but
where?

YELLOW TRIUMPH

Busy amazer of yellow and blue, the morning came
attended as if by several gods, and therefore a crazed
and bleaching sun in February, a sun as white and new
as piled snow. Lady of the name, it is you who drop
the gifts too soon, you to whom the whole sky opens
and shuts its eye in an ugly clouded wink, babies staying,
babies gathering under the shuddering fluorescents, in dark-
striped, shuttered rooms. Work calls, the spinning wheels
of the cash register, silver cart, stock stuttering wheel
of the neon O, all your job and the walk to work, the feeding,
stacking, paint-peeling bathroom, boyfriend hum and so.
Think, think, of the world going under in each
waxed-lemon moment, each geranium struggling to reflect
like the muddy lake in the park, light the lid withholds
from the god of the infant blink. Dogs come and go,
but it is you who hold the shuffled pile of everything
in your hands, and asleep to the TV, tag still on, how can
and must be so that all the eyes be bathed and soothed and
the perfect world be ready for puncture and wholly arrayed,
undropped, unpunched, unsmothered, unsick.

MAYTIME

That Maytime is the single biggest time
for water come crashing in, that leaves are beads,

then twisted knives, a man as if lime-treated
in belly, in shark, in skin so folded bones,

is not much proof, if then or now, that we
have made our mark on dirt or flesh or swim;

and thus I sit on sand, beached among the plums
that shed their silk-thin ivory coins to fray

from salt and grit suspended in expensed,
reneging waves, May's grim prospect that it's

inside a thing divided by hands, pulled grain
from grain; that leaves are cheap and wondrous

machines for trading me and sun to yet
more leaves; that the scars I make on sand and plum

bleed sand and plum, please, sit with me and wait
with back to the beating water's creatures, face

to the land's eaten face, that May and I can see ourselves
ground down, not much, ash-pollen in the mouth of the sea.

ROSEMARY
Rosmarinus officinalis

Remember, doctor, we all loved vacation, lived seaside
in its relentless reflected sun, its sucking, wet-dry
winds, membranous salt curing the never-lost leaves
you evergreened and almost needled. So if this break

lent itself to shoving trash into your mouth,
your heart choked with smokes and pinky hotdog skins,
then home was not a remedy. It was a maidless place
of thin light and pendulous, limpid water, and one grew leggy,

one lost head, and became a little petulant, vainer,
vaguer, inland. And exactly half dead in the
narrowing corridor of windowsill light, the nurses
ignore your lopped-off self, your affections of head and nerves,

the slippery, bitter place you've surely tried to bare
and clean, ready to be stitched with leaves. Nurses
serve to keep up the obstructions to blood and air, the thing
that forgets. They are no doctors. Were. Innards

through which the food and bad news might nudge
as if through a long-off, cheap screen door, slap bang
to your questions, the rules helpless, as if the kids

had already vacated and you were remembering
less expensive, more dutiful, veinier times. Are.

CURE

Cured of foresight and a body that
feels, a man finds himself
in his kitchen, which is also a forest.

A woman calls for him; this is his wife,
who considers it a place easy to negotiate,
though it seems full of hospital silver (this may

be the moonlight) and legs of growing, heavy
wood. It may be he answers, for the Romans
he's been reading to avoid the knife advise a cure

of hellebore in vinegar if the disease is alive,
horehound in wine if it's dead. He'd
never know where those things are,

and she would. The forest goes dark
and his legs give. Diagnosis: Always
something wrong, too soon. And now

comes metal, and now comes the wood.

GORGEOUS NORTH

Magnolia, throat too soon open to the fumbling fingers of beetles,
or closed in floodlights' saccharine solution, but hanging on
and worse for it, trees full of tossed-back, wine-stained gloves

to which the nurse said no you can't go: elegant or not, blood goes
    brown
on treated cotton, and from gut or gullet, bile is crafty as sin.
When *can* you go? When you won't pour forth, nor on

the steely ground. When you need none of nurse, cotton, skin,
shield and sheath to the squirrels' squalling selves outside,
the tree's bark slipping under their feet and petals falling

away, heavy, veined, and thick. But when if not then, Sister, when
your face is flush with your foe and nobility a kind of style,
your neck showing red against the white, a sting of pleasure

in being gone through, something new coming in.

BEES

STING

Is it instincts in the bridge of my nose; is it
aphids or sweat bees; is it wishes, stings
torn from their bodies and left in someone else;
switches cut from a willow and reddening someone
else's legs, twigs stripped from it; is it
a body ripped in half by the need to defend
the nest, pitiful, hung in a tree; a body
a hanging hole, hung by its wings, a dripping
viscous; a bullet's vicious sting that halves
your organ, haves your singing life while never
being seen, carrying in the microbes,
the little, quiet feasters that will really
bleed you, growing big, weeping, teeming
hives of themselves. Switched, you might wish,
for someone else; I might think, there could be worse things
inside oneself: halving and growing sick with no wound
to mark the entry, nothing left with to sting.

REQUEEN

Election time and the underlings wait
in the curtained wings: my girls will work
for me, they say, in wet and cold, and work
is dressing the aspirants up as prolific, fat layers,
egg-white cakes of delicious, thick sweetness:
teeth-white hair of a costume-party talk show host:
Yes, says Candidate 1, a worker can
come up here; look at me, I'm one—
And I look for the sugar shake and roll
into town, a kicking line of layer cakes
with legs, a well-lit office party, baby:
maybe Candidate 2, gleaming gold
with rings: smile the smile: the world is right
but might be righter: the world is damaged but might
not be so mean: damage
sweetening the best of things and people:
a crooked smile, the thinning hair is how:
you know the girls and by the girls the others
really love you: a cat and wasp
game to put your cake of makeup on for:
Candidates 3 and 4: and here is the sign
of true election: the clipped yes crippling wing.

SCOPA

You look like you know what it's like to save,
not quite conservative but enraged by the name factories
calling themselves breeders, hundreds of them
open with the same tag: 'Melissa,' 'Jessie,' 'Alison.'
Almost making you say hey, ladies, may I take a lump
of yellow for either miniature carry-on bag
and share the wealth of breeding, like the bees,
for it's always time for them, stroking their leg-hair for change,
like a little seed-money's all that's needed to make
an off-site bank; it's expedient, it's legal, conservationist
hoarding up of pollen that compounds into something
more. And so stopping the production's so sweet,
like freezing a bit of unneeded potential by eating it
or feeding it to your sweetheart's gorgeous
mouth; sure and somehow, 'Mr. Ian Hyde,' famous
hybrid maker, of course there will be like so much more
stuff for everyone, everyone being
not just bees but people and roses and viruses
who'd like to save up, who're saved in a way for those
who couldn't save themselves or see
the long range point of breeding miniature folios,
those who couldn't stay their luck to be breathing
for the clones they made and say the name of what
that before had always sort of guaranteed—like 'Sophie's Hope'—
like good, like gold, the same.

LAVENDER BLUE

The king bee droned interminably of his flat heart;
the queen sat fat and took it, music for
the dream of ruined honey, the whipped-up
fields of dill making it liquorish
and pickled. Who said it was ridiculous,
who said there is no king, no whip. No dill
or mind of queen or she. The queen sat
still and wasn't listening. You should call
your friends to work, said he, and meant that it
would make them king and warm to know that other
future queens worked forks for them and tore the ground
to scented shreds; it did surprise the candied
queen the way she quivered drones, the owned
blue shimmer of them crushing underfoot.
Though you couldn't listen to their groaning
dreams of ruling over others; they didn't know
that all that was was making more of them.
So dull to know. And still they would insist
that it was better watching whipping than the whipper.
Better drinker than the liquor. And queens
must be still, almost resisting asking over
and over who told them so.

WHIPPING-BEE

All through the whipping-bee, everyone dreamed up
their own bees: dining-bees with heavy silver,
a bee to admire a prodigal child, a caulking job,
a money-bee to counterfeit a mint
or to work the fields at night. People
whip-stitched round the edges of
a quilt of black and gold, raised the frame,
pressed apples from their skins, friends
at least, in willingness to raise and press
and skin, despite their illness of the fastest stitch,
a whisper and spit-house built for karma.
But the whipping-bee was different: people
weren't just labor, rather were the sum
of stings their tongues could make. That's all;
and whether you liked it from silk or needle, leather
or gilt, you knew how much you'd split.
You could not be surprised by the whipping-bee's
results: measured by your pleasure it meant
feeling sore and crabbed next day at home;
the kids announcing they were hitched;
no one able to find the sharpest blade
in the kitchen, chisel gone from the box.

HORSEFLESH

Like the stone spoon eyes of a man whose casket
bought and built says no I'm going down
to the track and will be long as I can go,
and lucky bornite cracked and ribmeat red
inside his pocket, he goes—or pushy elders
telling mothers horseflesh eaten from the bone,
between month one and two of eating flesh,
will make your child's conscience clean—this is how selfish
I have been, how ballerina and bloody toed
I've minced through what I got, ridden high
inside my pocket; uh-huh I used my knees
and a metal bit to push the best flesh hard
through sharp-rocked shoals and then forgot. Not
that I know any better. No I bored
to death expensive pros with every part
of myself I could butcher and scale and scold. So
I'd say I never gained a thing, even less than
the bloody old gambler pushing his luck or
the white bones spooned in the charnel house gravel
and cleaned by the meat bees in six days cold.

ROBBER BEE

Not a mechanic or a gracious host,
not your mop-up expert, your cold car block
or the hotwiring fingers, reluctant, rich nectar
or sharp mouthparts to cut through the bud to the chase;
whatever, ghostly, rob what you like: come
through a hole in the door; hold the whole place up; rip
the clothes and carpets for sugar and keys;
upend the bed and try and find what cost
the most; fix and eat a snack that no one can take;
check the sex and make of the enframed relatives
and vow to hit them next; break glassware and candlesticks.
It's dying in here. Here's cake. And wax. And rich
enough and weak, someone must be robbed,
the neighbors or yourself; the empty gun
to the temple; specialist without
the grace to take what's smoothly served
to everyone else— and what's left?
the blasted flowers drying up, the getaway
car stripped for parts and rusting helpless
in the bay. Everyone else is those
who walked in and stole what you had to rob; picked
it up. Flashed a sticky smile. Walked away.

SUPERS

Take the lawful fob on a watch away,
the hair bracelet, the after-dinner savory
and séance routine, you'll have the super-blue,

silver-white gold of an utterly modern snow
plus sun, reality show of what is money
when exposed: a mob of awful ideas

or honey-saving familial glue or an ungodly
law centrifuging white sugar at table away
from you, hiding the watch, the hair bracelet unplaited

and savaged. The sun on the divine Morris carpet may argue
this new time's old, but everyone knows that tired
and untrue morality play that no one can say

who has the blood to become supermodels or stars,
supermediums channeling the glamorous dead. For example.
One's mores and wit might bet on a wavy-grained nymph

of a nation, rich and blue-laked—then find it's her intuitive sister
or crook-toothed brother blowing the world away
with an ancestor's smile, an antique gun or two.

It could happen, even to one, and though
Supersedeas said once it couldn't be done,
it was at least once, the inner works of the watch lawlessly

crystalline crushed on the carpet and someone weeping,
betrayed in the hope that the hair would bind, the heir
step aside for the merit inherent in a younger

and ghost-sanctioned heroine. Last faith pinned
to the savory, that it might fill the family mouth of the man
fumbling with the gun's old safety and mumbling

at the intruder and who the hell are you?

CUCKOO

Cuckoo could be one of us, a should-that-did
and screw the gawkers who said it was way too big
or that the world was an open beak to fall
into. Simpletons. For summer's what
is coming, the old I'll escort you down
hot mouthside and you can clamber in;
you can come out damp and cynical
and dead, cooed to it by the very ones
who stole the bread you made; they left eggs
in the crib and nothing else. Led
themselves away to glitterfaced nights with waspy,
lethal, Batesian dates, injuring as
they did the reputation of our sting
by dressing up as us and never killing anyone:
a one-off, an id lost in the costume
bagging around the knees and making
the drive-by much less safe. I dressed to kill
and killed so that the rest of us didn't have to,
says the glitterfed and better date,
excellent in nest and empty-handed,
opening the sporty door of some convertible.
Come on, get in, it's for the good of everyone.

QUASISOCIETY
for my mother

Delete the social; it makes much sexier copy
that there's a queen, a boss, a mean girl running
things or being deleted, a king with pretty
georgette dreams of giving the capital back
and setting everyone up as artisans, everyone with
a home in the ground, everyone making and saving
what their children need and then leaving it to them.
These warm days are a little inherited lingerie,
a thin and faux silk moment for the has-everything
know-nothing, the so-far-so-good bumbler without any manners,
who keeps on stetting the sunny present and by
that yellow chemise thinks living will keep looking
great. But it's creased and slashed, full of incomprehensible straps
and snapped back behind where no one can reasonably reach.
Instead, the bees are not what's hidden, but what
we can see: gold-banking colonies, yes,
but also briefly females sharing a queenless nest,
so near a field of flowers' fabulous strapless numbers
that each of them will breed and eat,
and when the flowers strip, close up and leave.

WRATH OF THE BEE

She leaves the present defenceless in order to save the hereafter.

Wrath is the last suit to want for the hereafter,
desire for pardon haunting everyone
on earth and writhing round the waist,
the belt to close that sentimental baggy bathrobe.
But wrath is the strapless dress for draining riches
of their meaning; a smashed house means just more
light for the tight finery, bloodied face the jewelry
that pulls the thing off right; the cocktail lights
the blood with I will mend it later, but now
this necklace is made for cracking, now a scalding
bath is what I mean by wax. Try
to step aside and store forgiveness inside me.
You see how I fall·down and seethe your goodness,
ruined permanently. Now save that.

There is the conviction, for instance, that the vestal vintagers cannot endure the approach of the unchaste, above all of the adulterous. It would be surprising if the most rational beings that live with us on this incomprehensible globe were to attach so much importance to a trespass that is often very harmless.

Harmless knows the hopeless like a globe
most rational; if you cannot harm, you cannot
much of anything: not steal, not go
down for it, and never eat. Go home, disgusted
lovers say to one another, but home's
the problem. It's where the cuckolding beloved always is,
waiting in the trim sweaters unsuspecting
on their shelves, the dirty fork who doesn't
know what it's done wrong, lying outside
its plastic cell. And then hopeless,
it's all flat trespass, a toothless kind of waiting
to have the guts to smash up someone's stuff or die.
Because someone did to someone else what they said
they'd do to me alone. I recommend:
wield another sharp and furious creature
to sting yourself some remorse. Wait, I mean hope.

[Bees from the poor hives'] only thought is to perish on the outraged threshold, and, lean, shrunk, nimble, unrestrained, they defend it with unheard-of heroism and desperation. Therefore, the cautious beekeeper's...offering is a honey-comb. They come hastening up and then, the smoke assisting, they distend and intoxicate themselves: behold them reduced to helplessness like the rich burgesses of the plentiful cells.

Behold hope as an insect bitch, golden bones
for legs, wraith-wristed, of course, a parody of the fat
and feathered. Hope dressed like this innocent
incessant, flipping through the racks and wanting
nothing, including what she has. Unlike
the thick worsted I wore for lingering outside
the stores and staring in. No one knows
what she's worth or can get her to slow
afternoon of drink and drags. Enter her enemies and
let me tag my help, the Furies; I didn't
make them up. Winged and gorgeous,
they can binge and score and steal a scene.
Rich and whistlers, they know the tricks
to staying fit and fair and torturing. A little gold,
a little swing in your step, dizzy with
a bit of a cigarette, a newly vicious
suit, wristy pink and knife-creased. Plus
the shoplifting and the dieting. Helpless
sweetness not allowed, of course. But smoke
can be your sin and kin, your kiss after melting kiss.

POLYLECTY

It isn't a human situation, is it,
being the ignorant oligolege, blind fat
and choosy specialist, body made for its food
and the rest of the place a blur. We know. Don't we.
Any tragedy's a custom-made and leisurely tragedy,
not some cheap polylecty of grief
massed in the draining line of yellow desert
but the desert levied with one ugly but flowering flower.
Aren't we omnivorous. That is generalists
who can't eat sand but can swarm almost any scape
and specialize, *Lasioglossum lustrans,* all of us
Las Vegas in the distance, green lawns, anemones.
Had I some taste I'd say I'm a tragic
specialist whose food is dying, grievously
drying up. Thus increasingly
less of me. What. Am I the only one
who sees something light in that?

THE ANIMAL PARLIAMENT

FUR COATS
Red Coat with Black Fur Trim

So everyone's got a red coat with black fur trim.
Blood on the inside's blue, hair the thin thought
of some cells left over from the last onslaught of wind
and sun, mutant squirrels with bare tails that shiver
in the brain thinking grow, grow, grow. Who knows
what parts are leaving me now, an eternal bad market
that ought to have made its bid, bought and sold
whatever it needed that I stay whole. Or at least
that's what I said to grandmother in line
at the bank, bag quivering full of her faithless money,
hands enviable angora gloves, cupping the cold
between their thin fibers. Couldn't you say just
it was cold? I don't like losing my hair
to an internal cause? Wish for something
else: that money never cared for me,
I found a coat that used me to warm and move
its satin innards, made me a proud, poor blue-blood;
another ruddy unproductive cup; a shame, a sham, a hole.

Blue Fur Collar Coat

Dear blue animal, we thank you for
the fur that splays around our necks. And yet,
the sun that rims the clouds is just a cavity
in the making, so we cannot say with truth
we know your blueness gamboling near a frosted
lake or taking a furtive leak in a tropical alley.
Are we getting closer? The evidence says
against; the light says your hair is old and clumped,
from some dumb, dim place I can't remember,
some long-ago tearing of you from your muscles,
and you lay there poured, done on the snow.
We only have the skin to keep warm.
Or I've got it: I bet you slipped the noose, and
this is just your faux hair, the way my eyes are rimmed
with bone and therefore look only ahead:
I'm sorry. The cold tore down. I needed to get
in front of me, and I needed a way to go.

Vintage Black Coat with Fox Fur Buttons

So when some old-time vixen slim says so,
the camera winks its awful shattering light and life
is over: liquid and stiff we are forever
caught like 1929 cats, blind and angry, bodies
blurred and eyes revealed as naked, see-through
organs, odd and ugly cups of water,
shined on, dipped in, unsaved except for in
some fading box of photographs, the slick-haired
fox fur buttons on the black wool body
reanimated in the attic's dim,
impoverished tea party, condoms shoved into
the pockets, impossible to imagine grandmother's
slippery body, svelte, then wrecked, then gone
between the clothes: her teeth were fixed. Her laugh
was happy. Hair was thin. Like some pelt hung
on the fence, I can tell you nothing but inquire within:
the black wool, furred, and baggy bodied soul.

DRESSES OF THE WORLD

Dresses know the rules:
cover things up with a tender mouth,
the best ones sighing as if
nothing's inside, falling, shucked

rudely from the green, ugly stem.
In a dress I said no to the house
planted on a mudslide, fate
made sure by the bugs

scything themselves in the brown
grass, hardly ever wrong
about rain. The dress and I
ran back to the car, gauzed white

by our kid's sobs. A dress
held that same boy as he
learned the licit poses of grief:
in its lap, he went, bent

at the waist, from Hands
Outstretched to Collapse.
A dress that bit me in half.
And what am I? At best,

three-quarter sleeves, suspended
satin, torn and browning, too small.
And what do I mean by the world?
Another waist to choke on. Failure

to fall, when falling is the law.

JEWELRY

We pack it up. Yet the river
glitters; the simple leaves of the orchid
hang over the boardwalk from their
scarred, black stems. And
the island, strung to land by ferries;
I heard the hill has sprung new
waterfalls, dirty white leaks,
a new pounding of land and water
to something violent and nothing.
The doctor said for money hope
that what you are is better,
but this face was given to me
with brittle skin to get me across
the border. Just a little ugly,
the winter here, not spectacular,
nothing to get cross over. Tiny
things die around us in the litter,
soft and hard, but we
have these: stones: they are.

ISLAND BIOLOGY
for my father

1.

It's hard to imagine we were so mad
about the place, when all it did was laugh

at us: fields of yellow flowers tittering
in the wind, the sun's oily heat bubbling up,

and then the goats. We were there to see
the smeary sunsets, see the planes almost reach

us and then have to turn back. Or rather,
we were definitely the men, dropped off by the crew

that said we were infectious, and we begged
to go back to the ship as they rowed off,

go back to the storms, the parched drifting,
the wooden-winged swarm to the land mass.

2.

The rest seems like a long revenge,
on the diminishing goats, the virus at home,

which walked till it flew; the flowers,
turning their pained, ancient faces

toward the war of the bees and the wind.
The heat stops, like everything, the mockery

of a machine we built sighing, shuddering out
a smoke headline up where the planes are:

Why Are They Leaving? and we don't
know as the weather shuts its fist.

STILL LIFE WITH DATA

Though data on the page leaves behind
the snakes in cages, sheaves of paper, threadworms
stilled—I stilled—in formaldehyde, the thousand

gutted flowers—mine—bedevil the greenhouse floor
and raise a stink, the blood cleaned from the organ
before it's hung in spirits smears a slide,

and the pencil vomits awful numbers, litters
the reeking lab. My snake just died a day
ago, and still he smells, the milk-eyed frustration

of hunting for a year in circles with
a single tongue; the fork I cut
was cut to show that snakes with one are worse

than a human with an eye put out—put out,
the eye that's left behind will make the world a whole,
data that the snake's scarred tongue can never capture,

the left side of the world, his world, a stinking
little mouse. I waited for the snake, wholly rodent.
The fork I wiped—was wiped—from the lab's

black table. The data dumped onto the paper,
the hunted-for answer spat into the dumpster
that I tried to pull it from; was blinded

by the waste of reunited halves: the bloom
and worm, snake and fork, the whole and hungry mice.

SNOWSHOE HARE

Lepus americanus

1.

Hunt hares because they run and leap for you,
not rabbits, no, who freeze in plain sight,

brown fur hoping to hide itself in a lawn
of green, shivered to death like unturned leaves

in a cold snap. Planes graze the roofs
of the hard little house, floors to please even

the hard hare ma, dropping her ones on the ground
without nests, without the fur picked from her own

spare belly. She is not sorry. You and the hare
have the same disease: always make more

and destroy all the luscious green nibs of the saplings
before they are trees. The stunning living room's

paneled, angular view is always ruined by
the gaping field of the airport, the hunt for a place

bare of sound, rich with the lithe spines of grass.
For the house can't jump up and worm into you,

make you stay and raise anything here. The neighborhood
stretches its maw, a plain to be snapped up;

may choose; must choose; run,
you and your young disappear.

2.

And so inside the hare, bark and wood
are made to blood; faster-than-predator parasites

course through its organs, hang on, accrue,
spend from the inside the hare's crushed buds

and air and melted snow. In hare, lungs take on
a hue silvicultural, a burned-over timberland begun

again with worms, a held-together place
professional eaters call silverskin, the see-

through, you-taken-everywhere bag for muscles
and bones, hare become a soft-walled house in the wood,

the threads of whitened fur between the toes
that hang the hare above the sugar

drifts. Our houses made to grow and choke
each other, the nematodes to needle food

together, our blood and waste and water
shivering through the woods—and where is the animal?

—foot stitched to the ground that trembles there.

HOUND
Canis lupus familiaris

For those tired of the hunt, the hound
runs over the earth, the earth's familiar,

on toes to circle the muddied prints,
the hare, the fox: the wolf, the stag,

wound round the horses' legs
with glinting teeth; for whom? well, ask

the orbit above the hound, the world
slumped and dirty on the horses' backs,

the horses' feet hunting for the ground to devil
and crush. They say for blood and muscle

we seize and eat muscle and plants. Used to
it, raccoon-thieves, the demons of hounds,

circle above them in trees, their paws wound tight
to grip the branches, nails that do terrible

things to the wood. And around the wood,
jeering to catch him, the houses and cars,

his criminal palms—on what did he
use them?—above his head. For all of us,

loose the hounds to hunt the man.
My hands are my familiars.

COYOTE
Canis latrans

And as the coyote turns the cat to sweetness
in its mouth, a month-long stint of apricot
pit-, ant-filled scat, a month before of
birdseed, cricket, crappy sandwich; so,

don't turn your back; befriend them; grab
and wave a stick; the twenty doses meant to still
their little ones were killed inside coyote,
and outcome: snapping infant death: your indoor

dogs, and bitten, squalling children: dens
in rainpipes, basements, crawlspace, tenants' dumpsters:
a fed coyote is a dead—what? Since they ate
even the stinging sugar-eaters, since when

they couldn't eat they bred into your pets
a coyness, slipped behind the fence, endorphins,
dopamine sweeter than the kibble
                        —so what's to want?

With eyes like lanterns out by the latticed gate,
a future soft-tanned pelt pulls up
and moves to the city, deceitful little trot,
about to whelp and, honey, because the wolves

are shot and wildcats museumed and moth-torn,
the city, hareless, knows it's gone to them; omnivorous
I tell myself, so make yourself their home.

THE *ANIMAL PARLIAMENT* TALKS OF *WARRE*
after Margaret Cavendish

I. The *Serjeant* is *Dislike*

And breach the count, indeed that one should go
from home to death; so-and-so the judge's brother

had heard it on the radio that men
how many returned and killed their wives. It was

a kind of bird in bush they'd grown, with meat
for leaves: the wives and other men killed *them*. The Serjeant

knows as planes buzz-code the coppery sky,
the hedges that line the avenue breathe out

their domestic, unfeathering breath. From one to hundreds,
the Serjeant is and aggrievedly knows all the judge

and his brother, the blood and sleek-brown bottle of court.
A servant to hold their arms; so many said

they had died, and forensically they did seem over-
run. The bush in the Serjeant's hand bursts

into fleets of silver, hollow-boned, hating wings.
A message in unreadable binary: Yes,

at home, the bed is flayed. The clothes fly out
in sheaves. Let the Serjeant take care of your avenue,

muttering a seed in the beak of higher powers. Right

in the numbers. It isn't one. It isn't no.

II. The *Speaker* is *Love*

If love is but a chemic, scented breath,
the touch of mother's hair spun through the moss,
we will come into your house at night
and break your teeth with stones.

The man remembered nothing. But that
the corn went to the villagers, that stuff
he knew. The foreign birds cried low he knew,
shivered the fear through the woods.

Then love is the smell of something real, an idea,
the good corn, the village, the patriot man
with an animal sound we remember without
his name; the hairline rings of drought

in stumps a skewered, spun-out history of want;
the deformations of an acid mother-love
that speaks itself through villains, the roads, the rocks,
a gap-toothed grate who's teaching the water to run

and never break through all that hair and bones:
keep low, keep low, keep low.

III. The *Clerke* that writes down all is *Fear*

Note: if kids hate bugs and leaves we'll have the needful
things for war; the shelves are stocked with trucks
and girls: pink and brown, soft and hard;

the identical trying to spread their single selves.
Or when someone in the place can find a pen—
record that money and biology

decline the populations on their own
and leave the lucky, lovely, untouched few, just
kids, your speaker, here outside the dusty,

foreign gloom of your hometown, instore
a home of soft vanilla-scented plastic,
green-hard army men, unbroken from each

other, right, then we'll have a villain, then
the leaves will know they're chemical. So kids
hate bugs, hate green, and cannot keep their hands

off them—now, take this down: let's have the war
and then we'll open up the box of this grim clerk
and read what's resting soft and low behind

what's written. Hard numbers, code, detail
for what I need, I did. We may never be alone.
Clerk's a pen to lower the idea and make

it chemical. Your clerk is home.

GREENLAND
after "Foweles in the Frith"

Let me tell you I am ready for the news all the time
for the fires, failures, offspring's falls I know,
and the houses from the air looking like a kind, an insect

proof of building and decay. For the news I have
no defense but the definite article, a parasite love of getting what's
expected when you've packed your fat little ones away and

waited and then can tremble with the machine you're in
and fret the question can I survive so? My apocalypse saved
for last is all I ask and intend to do: go out and find the sun

behind the smoke and particled people and walk myself home;
but on and on the land goes, laced with dusty slowly dying wood
and buds sprung their flowers early and heavy with salt-

weight snow, green of their leaves overcoming their petals,
so a backwards adaptation: the kid-thoughts I thought
I had scuttled reverse me; epiphytic they are a part of my

goods, taking the brain to the animal there where the worm
noses up from the rising ground water; and welling its acids
against our skin, us pointlessly upward to drown in the rain;

though *o for an end* is not what we say; the plane still beached
when I with haunch and jaw to the disaster return, severity
of the storm untold even by snapped branches, unknown even

to the houses who lapped up the vines and grass with grave
flatworm abandon;   let not honeysuckle be
the first to know my darling, my only inside, my best of bone.

JOURNAL OF ARID ENVIRONMENTS

Sweet in the tea to cover the salt,
the equal seethings of sand and water,
dark green leaves' dominion all
over Georgia. The bacon in the pan
heaves like something almost dead,
past the walk-on-water index, extraneous
gravity, density, length. Insects surface
everywhere around the camp, this
sameness. Enough leaf, liquid, heat.
Meat and bread. Legs, arms, head,
blood, feet. To do and see things.
A garden of bristlecones is a word
and a word and a word and a word.
Sun to make water everywhere and
your daily exercise: walk with the lord.

GAS PUMP

Dog like customer: slunk around
the pump not half-paid up. Circling in,
the blue and gold-smeared day, as if
it worked, was given. Isn't; breaks
on us like the cloud of oil-collecting
bees in the southern night, their tongues
as slick and rich as the ground near spills.
Speciose, green, greasy without humans,
what then? it would be *organism*
the helm, and they could, machines
to make you a needle: full, self.
Could be: more of me, dogs, bees.
It is a value: down at the tomato stand:
hurt and ugly, but three for free.

NOTES

Tulips

All the poems in the first section are titled after the cultivar or
 selling names of tulips except for "Rosemary."

"Gordon Cooper" uses a variation of one of Cary Grant's lines
 from *Notorious*.

"Party" is based on a phrase from a sign outside a church.

"Cure" refers to several Roman treatments for parasites.

Bees

To requeen a hive is to replace an old queen bee with a younger
 queen.

"Scopa" features the cultivar names of roses.

Supers are the top part of modern hives used by bees to store
 honey.

All quotes from "The Wrath of the Bee" are from Maurice
 Maeterlinck's *The Double Garden* (1904).

In "Polylecty," a polylege is a generalist organism that can get its
 food from a number of different sources, and an oligolege is a
 specialist organism that can get its food from only one source
 (e.g., a bee who only visits one species of flower). *Lasioglossum
 lustrans* is a specialist species of bee that evolved from a
 generalist species of bee.

The Animal Parliament

"Still Life" with data is based on H. Kahmann's work in the 1930s
 with snake tongues.
"Journal of Arid Environments" takes its last line from a sign out-
 side a church.
"Gas Pump" takes its last line from a sign outside a tomato stand
 near Ithaca, New York.

ACKNOWLEDGEMENTS

Thank you to the editors of each of the following magazines for publishing these poems for the first time: *ecopoetics:* "Snowshoe Hare"; *Fence:* "Journal of Arid Environments"; *Gulf Coast:* "Hound"; *Indiana Review:* "Fur Coats"; *Indiana Review:* "Requeen" and "Polylecty"; *New Orleans Review:* "Cure"; *The New Republic* (August 5, 2003): "Maytime"; *Phoebe:* "Whipping Bee"; *Pleiades:* "Island Biology"; *Quarterly West:* "Gordon Cooper"; and "Red Georgette"; *Sycamore Review:* "Dresses of the World"; *Verse:* "Sting," "Robber Bee," and "Horseflesh"; *Volt:* "The Animal Parliament Talks of Warre."

Thank you also to Andrea Selch, David Kellogg, and Evie Shockley for their interest in the poems and for their work at Carolina Wren Press. Thank you to Peter Fallon, Mark Doty, Jorie Graham, Dean Young, Forrest Gander, Bill Manhire, Roger Gilbert, Bin Ramke, and especially Alice Fulton for their generous mentoring; to Amity Gaige, Tim Watt, Matthea Harvey, Rob Casper, Sam White, Gillian Kiley, Vivienne Plumb, Tim Croft, Gina Franco, Janet McCue, Karl Parker, Jasper Bernes, Gabriel Gudding, Joel Kuszai, Jonathan Skinner, Max Winter, Josh Corey, Theo Hummer, Ann Buechner, Matt Boone, Toni Wall Jaudon, Chris Nealon, and Lyrae Van Clief-Stefanon for good fellowship and good discernment. A special thanks to Kathleen Hughes and Sally Keith for their tireless support. My family—Mona and Greg Anderson and Amy Josephine Swanson—are part of every word here.

The book was designed by Lesley Landis Designs

Printed in the USA
CPSIA information can be obtained
at www.ICGtesting.com
JSHW082226140824
68134JS00015B/752

9 780932 112583